DEDICATION

This book is dedicated to my amazing wife, April, and my beautiful girls, Anaia and Charis. Thank you for encouraging and supporting me to keep making history in my lifetime.

HISTORY
—— IN THE ——
MAKING

*7 Keys to Making
History in Your Lifetime*

COREY TABOR

III Coaching, Austin, Texas

WWW.TRUEVINEPUBLISHING.ORG

History in the Making
Corey Tabor

Published by
True Vine Publishing Co.
810 Dominican Dr.
Nashville, TN 37228
www.TrueVinePublishing.org

Copyright © 2025 by Corey Tabor
ISBN: 978-1-968092-05-4 Paperback
ISBN: 978-1-968092-06-1 eBook

Printed in the United States of America—First printing.

FOREWORD

When Corey first told me about *History in the Making*, I knew right away it wasn't just another book; it was a calling. A conversation starter. A guidepost. Corey has always had a gift for connecting. In this work, he does something more: he challenges us to focus on our history, not as distant facts, but as the foundation of what we build next.

As someone committed to building strong families, strong communities, and a stronger future, whether through financial empowerment, mentorship, or faith, I believe in the power of truth to transform lives. That is what this book offers: an invitation to focus on truths rooted in love, boldness, and legacy.

The use and application of focus is one of the most underrated abilities we possess as human beings. We see karate students master this principle to demonstrate superhuman abilities yet seldom apply the powerful use of focus in our everyday lives. Focusing on the keys outlined in this work will kick the reader into overdrive in creating a life that is rich and fulfilling.

What Corey has written is both timely and timeless. He reminds us that we are all contributors to the unfolding story of our generation. That history isn't just something we read; it's something we make with every decision, every act of courage, and every moment we choose purpose over comfort.

I've seen firsthand the way Corey pours into people. His heart, his thoughtfulness, and his grit show up on every page. This book isn't about exalting the past; it's about learning from it, owning our part in the present, and taking responsibility for what's next.

Whether you're a student, a parent, a leader, or simply someone searching for clarity in chaotic times, this book is for you. It is a reminder that we're not just watching history unfold; we're creating it.

David S. Walker
President & CEO
Forthright Investment Partners

TABLE OF CONTENTS

INTRODUCTION

History is in the making.
History is yours for the taking.
You don't have to wait until you get real old
You can start right now and press for your goal

These are the lyrics to the chorus of a song I wrote over 10 years ago, as I was thinking about how I could speak to this generation about becoming history makers. I have always loved history because I knew I could learn a lot from others' struggles and successes to improve my life and the lives of others. Growing up, I spent a great deal of time with people who were older than me, partially because my father pastored churches made up of older people, but also because I was always interested in how they got to where they were in life. I was one of those kids who, many said, acted older than I was and had wisdom beyond my years. Sometimes, people referred to me as an old soul. The truth is, I saw something in the eyes of people who have been through life that I wanted. I saw depth in their past, peace about the present, and confidence in the future that I wanted. They knew life would not be perfect, but they knew they would make it.

As I entered middle school and high school, I noticed that I was strongest in subjects of English and History. I believe part of my success in those areas was based on my love for history and how literature often connected me to history. Through Texas History, I learned how my state was established and what makes it unique. Through US History, I became aware of our revolutionary development, our ugly racial past, and our commitment to seeking a better future for the upcoming generations. Through British Literature, I was able to travel across space and time to a place I thought I would never physically see, to learn from people I knew I would never meet. History was my connection to the past and the key to unlocking my future.

You have likely heard the famous quote: "If we don't learn from our past, we are doomed to repeat it." I appreciate the sentiment of this quote because it is focused on not repeating the negative experiences of our past, but as an optimist, I see history as a chance to learn from the positive and painful past experiences to gain an even more informed and enlightened future.

So, history is important to our past, our present, and our future.

As we discuss the concept of History in the Making, we need to define history in a way that will help us better understand what we are trying to make.

The Webster's Dictionary entry for history is as follows:

history

noun: his·to·ry \ 'his-t(ə-)rē \

Simple definition:

: the study of past events

: events of the past

: past events that relate to a particular subject, place, organization, etc.

Full definition:

1: tale, story

2 a: a chronological record of significant events (as affecting a nation or institution), often including an explanation of their causes

b: a treatise presenting systematically related natural phenomena

c: an account of a patient's medical background

d: an established record <a prisoner with a history of violence>

3: a branch of knowledge that records and explains past events <medieval history>

4 a: events that form the subject matter of a history

b: events of the past

c: one that is finished or done for <the winning streak was history> <you're history>

d: previous treatment, handling, or experience (as of a metal)

So, one word, "history," can have many meanings in the English language. The best definition for the focus of this book would be "tale or story." History is simply his story or her story. History is the stories that make up our lives and how those stories intermingle to bring about a shared experience that impacts our lives.

On Tuesday, November 4, 2008, then the junior senator Barack Obama from Illinois was elected by the American people as the first U.S. president of African descent. I remember lying on the couch in the apartment my wife and I were renting. I had fallen asleep waiting for the results of the election, struggling to reconcile what I had seen in history and what many said could possibly have happened in history that evening. As an African American boy growing up in West Texas, I was always taught to believe we could be anything in the world except the president of the United States. I never thought I would see it happen in my lifetime.

As the night continued on, as local and state election results were coming in, I was tuned in to CNN, waiting for the results from Wolf Blitzer, knowing that CNN would likely not report the results until they were definite due to the challenge that occurred in reporting that Al Gore won the presidency in 2000, to later have to report that George W. Bush was elected as president.

As I rolled over and rubbed my eyes while awaking from an unexpected nap, I saw a large image of Barack Obama on the big media wall behind Wolf Blitzer as he announced that Barack Obama had secured enough delegates to be elected as President of the United States of America. Tears filled my eyes, and I ran into our bedroom, with my hands on my head, looked my wife in the eyes, and said, "It happened! It happened! He won!" The next phrase moved me to deep emotion as I said our child would likely be born into this nation under an African American president. I could not believe it. I was in shock. I was overwhelmed.

The next morning, I got on my computer and booked two flights to Washington, D.C., for the inauguration. I did not know if I would be able to get a formal ticket to officially attend the inauguration, but I knew I had to be in the city with the love of my life to witness this historical moment. History happens in moments that must be seized to maximize the historical moment in your life.

Over two months later, we flew to Washington, D.C., and, when we arrived, we saw people from all over the country and the world who had come to our nation's capital to witness history. I saw older African American women with walkers who likely marched for voting rights in the 1960s. I saw military personnel who, for the first time, would be serving under an African American commander-in-chief. I saw former college classmates from the University of Texas who were there to witness this moment in history.

As we lined Pennsylvania Avenue and watched the presidential motorcade pass us by, and as we walked into our designated area as a result of tickets my friend David Hanke secured for me and my wife, I was in awe. We watched the inaugural processional of representatives, senators, and past presidents. We all anticipated that epic moment when Michelle Obama walked out after Sasha and Malia, and, finally, President-elect Barack Obama took the stage. As I stood in the bitter cold with the love of my life on my left and one of my closest friends on my right, I inhaled that moment in history like the brisk air of the Colorado mountains. It felt pure, it felt deep, it felt right.

On January 20, 2009, I witnessed history as President Barack Obama placed his right hand on President Abraham Lincoln's inaugural Bible and was sworn in as the 44th president of the United States. On that day, my life changed forever. I believed in our nation's ability to move beyond the ugliness of our racial past to a hopeful, reconciled future. History was in the making. On that day, President Obama's story and my story were intertwined with the stories of over 69 million Americans who voted for him and over a million Americans who made their way to our nation's capital to view this historic moment.

History is "his story" or "her story." The story I've shared, in all its detail, is now a part of the history I was able to make by voting in the 2008 election and attending the inauguration. It is a story I will pass on to my children and grandchildren to let them know the impact that this story had on my life and my generation.

This book is entitled *History in the Making: 7 Keys to Making History in Your Lifetime.* The focus of this book is to provide seven principles that I have learned over the last 30 years that have allowed me to make history in various areas of my life. I believe if you are able to apply these principles to your life, your story can become one that is considered historical by your friends, family, and beyond. So join me on a journey, and let's make history together.

CHAPTER 1

7 Keys to Making History in Your Lifetime

I was born on December 20, 1976, in Great Falls, Montana, at Deaconess Hospital. I was born to my father, Samuel Earl Tabor, who was serving in the Air Force, and to my mother, Carrie Hazel Tabor, a caregiver to children and later to adult women with mental disabilities. By the time I was born, my parents had been married for seven years and already had my brother, Samuel Troy Tabor, in August of 1974. My mother experienced five total miscarriages in this order: four miscarriages, followed by carrying my brother Troy to term, followed by another miscarriage, and then finally she had me.

Knowing our family history deeply spoke to me as a child growing up. I knew that I was meant to be here. I could have easily been one of my siblings who did not survive. This sense of purpose and destiny was prevalent in my upbringing as I experienced the joy of growing and learning in the home of a father who also served as a pastor in the Church of God in Christ, the largest African American Pentecostal denomination in America.

Being a preacher's kid (often referred to as a PK) had many challenges. For the first seven years of my life, I attended church nightly. In the years that followed, I traveled 60 to 90 miles three times a week to attend services. I was simply expected to either be perfect or unruly, depending on one's perspective and past experiences with PKs.

With all the challenges that came with the role of being a preacher's kid, the benefits were exponential. I was raised by parents who believed in me and supported me fully based on the simple fact that I was their child and not based on my performance. I was raised in an environment where character and integrity mattered and were cultivated. I was raised to be confident in my abilities and the call I had to maximize them to make the world a better place.

With all this in mind, I can honestly say I did not start out trying to make history. I was not one of those kids who grew up wanting to be the first Black president or the doctor who would cure cancer. What I wanted most was to make a difference. Making a difference became a passion of mine early in life. I believed I was given certain gifts and abilities to make a difference in the lives of others, so I endeavored toward that end, and the byproduct became me making history.

I hope you hear my heart when I say I am not writing this as a memoir of my life or as a brag sheet of my accomplishments. I am writing this book as a tool to help you see how to maximize your life, to make your story one that leaves a lasting impact— one of which you, your family, and your community can always be proud.

7 Keys to Making History in Your Lifetime

There are 2 "D's" connected to 5 "E's" that will help you make history. They are as follows:

1. DISCIPLINE - The ability to say "yes"!
2. DECISION - The ability to say "no" so you can say yes to something else.
3. EXCELLENCE - Doing the best you can with what you have.
4. EFFORT - Doing the best you can when you don't have to.
5. EXPECTATION MANAGEMENT - Learning to manage your expectations, leading to satisfaction or surprise more than disappointment.
6. EDUCATION - Learning how to learn.
7. EXPERIENCE - Learning from your experiences to maximize your education.

In this book, I will spend one chapter on each of these seven principles, explaining how they apply to you making history in your lifetime, as well as providing historical examples of others who have applied these principles to their lives. Throughout the book, I will weave in my story at various points to share how these principles have helped me make history in my lifetime. We will end each chapter with reflection questions that can be used for personal reflection as you consider how to apply these principles to your life.

I truly believe that if you put these seven principles into practice, your life will be more meaningful and impactful in ways that will lead to history-making for years to come. You may be like I was as a kid, not specifically wanting to be famous or known, but I believe all of us have an innate desire to make a difference. Whatever motivation you need to move forward in this area of your life, I urge you to find it and use it as fuel to be who you were created to be and do what you were created to do.

CHAPTER 2
Decision
The ability to say yes

Making history in your lifetime begins with making a decision—the ability to say yes. You have to say yes to what you want to do, to what you want to be, and to what you want to have or experience in life. Too often, people carry dreams and desires in their hearts without giving themselves permission to say yes. They may even envision a greater future or plan for a better tomorrow, yet still hold back from that simple decision.

Growing up, I was one of those kids who believed my parents could do anything I asked of them if I gave them the opportunity to say yes. I never said no to myself; I made them tell me no, because I assumed if they could do it, they would. My brother, on the other hand, often talked himself out of asking. He assumed he already knew their situation and believed they would say no.

Our experiences growing up were very different. I asked for things he thought our parents could not do, only to discover they were often possible if he had simply asked. We had the same parents but very different perspectives on what they could provide. Learning to say yes to what you want in life works the same way. You can think of every reason it cannot happen, or you can give yourself permission to say yes and see what unfolds. Saying yes is not a guarantee that you will make history in your lifetime, but it is the starting line.

I ran cross country and track in middle and high school. My races ranged from one to three distances. There was always a huge set of butterflies in my stomach as the starter called those famous words: "On your mark . . . get set . . . go!" The first two words represent the visions, dreams, and desires for your life. You have a mark, your starting point. You have a set, your beginning goal. But ultimately, you have to decide to go.

At one track meet, I remember an athlete who was really nervous about his race. It was his first time competing in high school. All his practice runs had been with teammates, and the starts were informal. He was used to casual beginnings, but this time was different. A few hundred people were watching, his friends were spread across the staggered starting lines, and this race actually counted. He had been calm in practice, but when it came to starting a race that mattered, he was visibly shaken.

For many of us, that is the same mindset. We can say yes when we are just imagining or considering something life-changing, but when the moment comes to actually begin, fear often cripples us. The result is a delayed yes or even a denied yes. We cannot control what others say about our desire to make a difference in our lives and in the lives of others. But we can control what we say to ourselves. The power is in your mind, and ultimately in your mouth, to boldly say yes, even when it feels unnerving.

Growing up, I watched the University of Texas football team play games every Saturday. I was an avid football fan and especially enjoyed watching my Texas Longhorns. One year, my parents took us to Austin, Texas, to visit my aunt and uncle, who lived on the east side of the city. While driving down Interstate 35, we elevated on what Austinites know as the upper deck. I looked over to my right and saw the University of Texas campus at Austin.

The large, sprawling campus seemed so intriguing. Then we passed the stadium, where the Longhorns were playing the Penn State Nittany Lions. The stadium was filled from top to bottom. I could see fans sitting in seats hundreds of feet in the air. I could hear the chant, "Texas ... Fight." I was fascinated by this place that carried a great deal of mystique. In my mind, I remember thinking, *What would it be like to go to college there?*

Over the years, I discounted the idea as just a passing thought. But as I prepared to graduate from high school, I was fortunate to be accepted into a number of local schools, including Abilene Christian University and Hardin-Simmons University. I pondered where I would pursue my college education. At first, I thought it made sense to stay in Abilene, where I had grown up, a small town in West Texas with about 110,000 people. I was well known, had great connections, and plenty of support. I was offered scholarships to attend both universities and was even offered a full scholarship to one.

As I thought about the idea of staying in Abilene, it seemed that it would be too easy to remain in town while going to college. I would have so many people who could help me and give me an advantage in school and in life. I had established relationships with the mayor, the city council, and my state congressmen. I was co-hosting a children's television show on a local affiliate. I was the speech team president, the student body president, and had even been crowned homecoming king that fall. I was living the dream life as a senior. Everything that could have gone well had gone well.

The more I pondered this decision, the more I felt I needed to take the risk of leaving my hometown—where I was comfortable, known, and accepted—to move to Austin and attend one of the largest universities in the United States. At the time, the University of Texas had nearly 50,000 students and more than 15,000 faculty and staff. This place was a city in itself, nearly half the size of my hometown.

Austin was completely different from where I grew up. It was more liberal politically, religiously, and socially. People looked different, sounded different, and acted differently from what I had grown accustomed to for the last 16 years of my life.

In the end, I decided to leave home and pursue my education at the University of Texas. Many people tried to convince me that my choice was a mistake. They warned me that I would be "weeded out" of classes because some freshman courses had as many as 500 students. They told me I would not find people who affirmed my faith or accepted me for who I was. But in my heart of hearts, I knew I was making the right decision. I remembered that moment as a child riding on the upper deck in Austin, looking over at the campus and wondering what it would be like to go to school there. I realized I could not leave that question unanswered.

So I said yes to leaving my parents, yes to leaving my comfort zone, and yes to ignoring the naysayers and doubters. I had to be willing to say yes to experience what I believed would be a great educational opportunity to prepare for my future. On the morning of July 16, 1995, I loaded up my orange 1979 Toyota Corolla, said goodbye to my parents at their church, and drove to Austin, Texas, to begin my collegiate career.

To be honest, I was excited, but more than that, I was terrified. I didn't know if I would be smart enough. Everyone who was attending UT seemed intelligent and accomplished. I was afraid people would not like me or accept me for who I was. I was even intimidated by students from larger cities because of rumors I had heard about crime and city life. I feared failure and worried I might end up returning home to attend one of the colleges in my hometown.

Fear was prevalent, but it was not prevailing. I did it afraid. In less than one week, I had made new friends who would become lifelong companions. I discovered gifts and abilities I had never fully tapped into and found ways to use them to contribute to the world. Saying yes to attending UT changed my life and the lives of many others—something I will share more about later in this book.

The Rev. Dr. Martin Luther King Jr. had a great many choices to make early in his life. He was raised as the son of a pastor and was extremely intelligent and gifted. At age 15, Morehouse College lacked the desired enrollment numbers, so it offered open admission to anyone who could score high enough on the entrance exams. Young Martin was not as big as the young men applying to Morehouse, but he knew he had a desire to pursue his education and be equipped for his future. He said yes to taking the admissions exam and was accepted. He said yes to enrolling in Morehouse College. He said yes to graduating on time and enrolling in graduate school. By the time he was 26 years old, he had completed his doctorate at Boston University, started a family, and was prepared to make a difference in the world.

When Rosa Parks sat down in the front of that now-infamous bus—a catalytic moment in the civil rights movement—Dr. King was ready to stand up and lead our nation toward improved civil rights. Throughout his life, he kept saying yes: yes to protesting, yes to giving speeches, yes to organizing activists, and yes to risking his life. Dr. King made the decision to say yes repeatedly, and as a result, he will forever live on in American and world history.

Ultimately, to get where you want to be in life, you must begin by permitting yourself to say yes. Say yes to considering a new relationship, even though you were hurt in the last one. Say yes to re-enrolling in college, even though you dropped out a year or two ago. Say yes to becoming financially independent, even though everyone else expects you to work a job. Say yes and see what happens. Your yes follows the passion you have for making a difference in the world.

I don't want you lying on your deathbed years from now saying, "I wish I had asked her out," or "I wish I had gone back for my master's degree," or "I wish I had started my own business." The choice is up to you. Make the decision and say yes!

CHAPTER 3
DISCIPLINE

The ability to say no, so you can say yes to something else.

We live in a society where the word *discipline* has almost become a curse word, so to speak. When told that children are being disciplined in school, some parents become angry at the teacher instead of considering the possible negative behavior of their child. When pulled over by a police officer for speeding, many will protest and debate the charge, knowing they broke the law, but upset that they were caught. When called by a creditor who is owed money, people often become angry and defensive, even though they signed receipts stating, "I agree to pay back all charges charged to this account."

By nature, we typically do not like discipline because it is not always a pleasant experience. Whether being disciplined by others or choosing discipline for ourselves, it can feel uncomfortable.

Yet people who make history have found a way to discipline themselves, even if only for a season, in order to create the history they are remembered for.

I define discipline as the ability to say no so that you can say yes to something else. In a world where everyone receives a participation trophy and many are approved for loans they cannot truly afford, the answer no is one we often do not want to give ourselves, much less hear from others. For this reason, we must cultivate the practice of saying no if we want to be able to say yes to something greater.

One of the areas I am most fascinated with when it comes to discipline is health and wellness. Companies like Weight Watchers make millions of dollars each year holding people accountable for disciplined eating habits. We do not have to pay a company to say no if we are disciplined in our own habits. Still, if we have developed a pattern of eating whatever we want and engaging in little exercise, then to accomplish the goal of losing weight and, more importantly, being healthy, we may need someone to help us practice the discipline of maintaining our health.

I know a few individuals who are professional athletes. They are naturally gifted, but as they move into the professional stage of their careers, natural ability alone is no longer enough to excel. They have to engage in extreme levels of discipline to be the best they can be. I happen to know history maker Sanya Richards-Ross, who ran the 400-meter dash and the mile relay for the United States track team. One of the disciplines she practiced for years was completing at least 1,000 sit-ups per day. She eats healthy with a few cheat meals here and there, and her workouts are intense.

Many people see her posts on Facebook showing what I call abs of steel and think, *It must be nice to spend all day training with a personal trainer. I could be in that kind of shape if it was my job and I had a trainer.* The envy, jealousy, and strife often build as they compare her body to their "normal" body. To be honest, most would not be willing to embrace the discipline of training for a living or following every directive from a trainer to prepare for the biggest races of her life. She has given her life to her profession and made countless adjustments to accomplish her goal of being a world champion and Olympic champion. She not only said yes to pursuing a career in track, but she also said no to other things that would have kept her from accomplishing that goal. You can read more about her journey in her books *Run with Me: The Story of a U.S. Olympic Champion* and *Chasing Grace: What the Quarter Mile Has Taught Me About God and Life.*

Often, discipline decisions are precipitated by catalytic events that drive us toward change. We may get a negative report from the doctor saying we have the onset of diabetes, and so we need to limit our sugar intake, decrease our belly fat, and increase our water consumption. The fear of diabetes scares us into considering the discipline it will take to remain healthy for ourselves and our families. We may be laid off from a job without having established the recommended three to six months of savings, so we resolve to put our finances in order and begin saving when we find our next job. We may end a relationship in a painful breakup where we compromise our values and purpose to avoid loneliness. After realizing that sacrifice did not pay off, we decide to discipline ourselves and live the principled life we always wanted to live.

The catalytic events are a great jump start to the motivation needed to practice discipline, but often they are not enough to maintain it. Three weeks after the doctor's appointment, we attend a family dinner, and when the desserts are lined across the kitchen counter, we indulge beyond our limits. We start making money again after landing another job, only to begin spending 98 percent of our income because we feel we deserve it. We enter another toxic relationship because, after three months of principled living, we are lonely. The *no* of what we want is not greater than the *yes* of what we need.

How can we be more disciplined to say no to something so we can say yes to something else? I have three recommendations to practice the discipline needed to make history in your lifetime:

Right Motives

Our motives are the driving force for much of what we do. The right motives lead to intrinsic motivation, which becomes the fuel to push ourselves beyond our comfort zone so that we accomplish our goals. When our motives are based on a desire to "one-up" someone or to get back at someone who hurt us, the motivation often dissipates because that motive is external, and the passion can waver or fade.

If our motive is simply to be rich so we can drive a nice car, live in a big house, and inspire envy, we may accomplish the goal yet feel unfulfilled. After a while, the car is no longer nice enough, the house no longer big enough, and the people we wanted to impress are no longer impressed. So we keep upgrading just to stay motivated.

The best and most lasting motives are those that are intrinsic and rooted in a desire to affect others positively. Negative energy never produces positive, long-term motivation.

Group Accountability

We need someone—or often a group of people— to hold us accountable for accomplishing our goals.

The thousands of dollars I paid the University of Texas at Austin is an example of group accountability. Honestly, I could have gone online and downloaded every syllabus of the classes required for my degree. I could have checked out all the required books from the library. I could have even sat in on many of the classes and listened to the lectures without enrolling. But I was not disciplined enough to do that on my own for four or five years.

So I paid the university to provide professors who would give deadlines, assignments, and grades to hold me accountable for learning. Since its founding in 1883, the university has proven that it does a better job of keeping people responsible for learning than they are typically capable of doing themselves.

So, when I look at my degree every day in my office, I am looking at a piece of paper that cost me a lot of "paper," so to speak, because I was not disciplined enough to write the papers and read the books on my own. I needed the investment of my money and the structure of the university to hold me accountable for getting the information I needed to secure my degree. Now I realize that most employers would not have hired me without the degree, since most of the jobs where I have worked required at least a bachelor's degree. But the real reason I paid the university was to provide that group accountability that would motivate me to learn.

You can create group accountability by joining a class at the gym or through a book club. You can have stand-up meetings each week at work to report on your progress or hold weekly family meetings with your spouse and children. The key is to ensure that others are holding you accountable for reaching your goals and for making the history you are meant to make.

A Bigger Yes Than Your No

Every day, we face choices about whether to say yes or no to opportunities in life. If our yes is not bigger than our no, our disciplined no will not last long. As I mentioned earlier, I was a long-distance runner in high school. I was on the varsity track team my freshman year and the varsity track and cross country teams my sophomore year, where I finished second in the district championship and in the top thirty-five at the regional championships. During that same year, I was diagnosed with exercise-induced asthma, which required me to use one inhaler an hour before I ran and a different inhaler right after.

Throughout my sophomore year, I weighed my motives for running by remembering why I had started in the first place. I became interested in running while playing Pop Warner football at nine years old.

My coach had our team run a mile every day after practice in the scorching West Texas heat. I would always finish first on our team with some ease, so one day he asked me if I had ever considered running cross country. I told him I did not even know what it was. I researched and discovered it meant running two- to three-mile races on natural paths with various levels of terrain. After learning more, I decided to join the team and did well. I enjoyed running and was successful until I was diagnosed with exercise-induced asthma.

In addition to the asthma diagnosis, my cross-country coach was moving to Eastern Africa to become a missionary, and a number of my friends were considering leaving the team. All of these factors weighed heavily on me at the time.

One catalytic event that helped me make my final decision was not a painful experience but a positive one. Rice University, one of the best academic universities in the country, was interested in offering me a scholarship to run cross country and track in college. I had an uncle who played college football, and I often noticed the college track runners at our local meets. I realized that I wanted to go to college, but I did not want to be a student-athlete. I wanted to go to college on an academic scholarship. I did not want to have to run to get my education.

After much consideration, I decided not to run on the track and cross country teams in my junior and senior years because my *yes* to running was not bigger than my *no* to running forty-five miles a week for practice. My *yes* to academics was bigger than my *yes* to athletics.

I decided to join the speech team and continued to advance in my Advanced Placement academic plan while serving on the student council. By my senior year, I was student body president—a historical achievement, since not many African Americans had served in that role before. As a speech team member, I advanced to the state semifinals in original oratory at the Texas Forensic Association State Speech Tournament. No one from my school had ever accomplished this feat before. I was making history because I was disciplined enough to leave athletics behind and pursue an academic scholarship to attend college. I earned eight scholarships, which paid for my first year and supplemented the remainder of my educational costs.

Where you want to go in life will take a great deal of discipline. If you want to be a history maker, discipline must become your friend and not your enemy. You may need to say no to playing video games so you can finish your homework. You might need to say no to sleeping in so you can say yes to being at work on time. You may have to say no to an unhealthy relationship so you can say yes to healthy self-esteem. History makers are committed to discipline by saying no to something so they can say yes to something greater.

CHAPTER 4
EXCELLENCE

Doing the best you can with what you have

We live in a society that is stuck in the comparison trap. We compare our lives to those we see on social media. We compare our gifts to people at work or in our community. The challenge with the comparison trap is that we are comparing two original people who cannot be the same. Comparison keeps us from being our best selves because it measures our lives against a false standard: someone else's life. You were not given what others were given; you were given what you have—your appearance, your gifts, your abilities, and your experiences. Excellence does not mean being the best; it means doing the best with what you have.

To do the best with what you have, you first need to assess what you have. I encourage you to take an inventory of who you are. In my book *Prioritize for*

Your Purpose: Ordering Your Life to Be Extraordinary, I wrote about a three-step process for discovering your purpose.

1. **Know your spirit.** This focuses on your faith, if you are a person of faith, as well as your conscience, values, and belief systems.
2. **Know yourself.** This includes assessing your gifts, abilities, acquired skills, passions, personality, and experiences. All of these combine to make up who you are.
3. **Know your season.** Your purpose will be lived out differently in each season of your life.

In getting to know yourself, I recommend these three simple steps to help you pursue excellence as a history maker.

<u>Acknowledge Who You Are</u>

You get to acknowledge who you are by exploring all the things that make you you. I encourage you to complete a personality assessment such as the Myers-Briggs Type Indicator, DiSC, StrengthsFinder, or the Enneagram. These cannot tell you who you are in a vacuum, but they can provide language to affirm who you are. These assessments are best taken after the age of twenty-five, once the prefrontal cortex of the brain is fully formed and you have lived through some experiences.

In addition to assessments, it is wise to observe your life through your experiences. Answering a survey based on who you want to be rather than who you are can be misleading. Checking your actual experiences helps confirm the results. For example, if you want to be outgoing, you may answer as if you are. Yet when you look at your life, you realize you spend most of your time alone at home. In this case, your experiences do not line up with the assessment.

Accept Who You Are

Once you acknowledge who you are, you need to accept who you are. This means embracing your personality, gifts, abilities, experiences, and passions. You make a decision not to change who you are at your core. You may adjust and grow in some areas to become more effective, but you accept who you are.

For example, you may not be a great public speaker by nature, but you can improve through training and practice. Accepting who you are means admitting that public speaking is not a natural skill for you. This frees you to seek training and practice without denying your limitations. Accepting who you are is vital to living in excellence.

Appreciate Who You Are

Finally, you learn to appreciate who you are. To appreciate can also mean to celebrate. Celebrate what makes you happy. Celebrate what brings you joy.

Celebrate what makes you unique and allows you to add value to the world. Appreciating who you are means not apologizing for who you are but embracing it fully.

I am outgoing, meaning I love to be around people. I am also an extrovert, which means I gain energy from being around people. Some people are one or the other, but many are not both. So I do not apologize for hosting get-togethers at my house or going to a football game with one hundred thousand people instead of watching it at home on my big screen. I have learned to acknowledge, accept, and appreciate who I am, which allows me to be fully myself in the world.

Living in Excellence

Once you know who you are and what you have, you can live in excellence, because now you can do your best with what you have. In high school, I was a driven, motivated perfectionist who wanted my hair to have a great edge and rolling waves every week. I would spend hours in the mirror trying to look just right. I would iron my shirts and pants, ensuring my creases were sharp and my outfit was the perfect mix of cool and preppy. I wanted to write the perfect paper and give the perfect speech.

As I stated earlier, I was strong in English and history but not as strong in math and science. Doing my best with what I had looked different in each subject. I could earn A's fairly easily in English and history, but excellence in math or science might have been a B. When I was in high school, taking an honors or AP course allowed me to bump my grade up ten points for enrolling in a more challenging class. Excellence for me meant taking the harder course, even if my grade was lower, because I knew it would prepare me for the level of academic rigor I would face in college.

Oprah Winfrey is now known as one of the most influential media moguls in the world, but she did not start that way. She was born on January 29, 1954, in Kosciusko, Mississippi, in the segregated South—the same year as the landmark Supreme Court case *Brown v. Board of Education*, which overturned the "separate but equal" doctrine by declaring segregation in public schools unconstitutional. Yet it took years before schools in the South were fully integrated.

At six years old, she moved to Milwaukee, Wisconsin, to live with her mother. Later, in her early teens, she moved to Nashville to live with her father. She faced many challenges growing up, including being teased and even molested, but she did not let where she came from or what she endured stop her from doing her best.

She received a full scholarship to Tennessee State University but left to pursue a career in broadcasting. She eventually earned her degree in 1986, at the age of thirty-two. At nineteen, she became a news anchor for a CBS television station in Nashville and later worked as a reporter and co-anchor for an ABC affiliate in Baltimore. She eventually moved to Chicago to host *AM Chicago,* which was later renamed *The Oprah Winfrey Show.* It became the highest-rated talk show in the United States for twenty-five years.

She also acted in critically acclaimed films and television shows, including *The Color Purple* and *Selma.* She formed her own production company, Harpo Productions, which produces films and television shows. Her publications have included *O, The Oprah Magazine,* and Oprah's Book Club.

She was the first African American woman to become a billionaire through her own endeavors. She has engaged in philanthropy through Oprah's Angel Network and opened a forty-million-dollar school for disadvantaged girls in South Africa. The list of her accomplishments could fill an entire book of its own.

Oprah was often criticized for how she looked early in her career. Some thought her skin tone was too dark for television. She has been very open about her challenges with eating, health, and fluctuating weight. She has been criticized for never marrying

46

her longtime partner, Stedman Graham. You may not agree with every path she has taken or the way she has lived her life, but you cannot deny that she has chosen to live with excellence. She did the best she could with what she had. She did not let growing up in the South stop her from pursuing her dreams. She did not allow the limitations others tried to place on her to keep her from becoming the person she wanted to be.

As you acknowledge, accept, and appreciate who you are, you have the opportunity to choose excellence every day by doing the best you can with what you have. You may not have the education you want, but you have some education—so do the best you can with it. You may not have the marriage or family you desire, but do the best you can with what you have. You may not be working at the company you want or making the amount of money you would like, but do the best you can with what you have and watch how it separates you from others. History makers consistently choose excellence.

CHAPTER 5

EFFORT

Doing the best you can, even when you don't have to.

Effort distinguishes extraordinary lives from ordinary lives. Most people will do the best they can when they have to. They will cram for an exam or run as fast as they can in a track meet. But I define effort as doing the best you can, even when you do not have to.

When I entered the University of Texas, our orientation advisors told us, "Look to your left and look to your right; next year, one of you will not be here." At first, I thought they were being harsh and trying to scare us into transferring to a smaller school. There are many reasons why someone might not matriculate or graduate from a school like UT. With fifty thousand students, and many first-year classes holding five hundred or more, it can be overwhelming. Everyone who is accepted into UT is smart enough to complete the degree; some simply lack effort. A 1600 SAT score does not guarantee success, because it takes effort to get the job done.

Someone with a 1600 SAT score who does not attend class or complete their homework will find themselves on academic probation and eventually fail out. In my freshman year, I took a U.S. history class that was the typical five-hundred-person lecture for freshmen and sophomores. On the first day, the room was filled to capacity. By the third week, only two-thirds of the students were still attending. By the end of the semester, half the students remained.

When finals season came around, I would see students coming back to class to attend review sessions so they could prepare for the exam. But they had missed so much of the instruction, and many had not read the assignments. At that point, they had a fifty-fifty chance of passing the class, depending on how well they could guess multiple-choice questions and write a short answer that was complex enough to impress a teaching assistant grading the test. Effort was the difference between failing and succeeding.

Joseph Mosley was my best friend in college. We were roommates for two years at the University of Texas at Austin, so I was able to watch how he managed his opportunity at such a prestigious school. Joseph had been valedictorian in high school, though he did not have the highest standardized test scores. He studied radio, television, and film in the College of Communications at UT. He joined Innervisions Gospel Choir and later Gamma Phi Delta Christian Fraternity. Over his time at UT, he held leadership positions in both organizations.

He was disciplined and focused on excelling in his academics. Most Friday nights, my friends and I would hang out, go to the movies, or go out to eat. We wanted to figuratively let our hair down for the week and relax. Joseph, however, was different. He saw Friday nights as the quietest nights to study. UT has a six-story library called the Perry-Castañeda Library, affectionately known as the PCL. On each level of the library were study rooms for group projects or problem-solving. There were also quiet spaces between the stacks of books, which we simply called "the stacks." Most students studied in one of these two areas. Joseph discovered the basement was among the quietest places in the library, with few distractions from people walking, talking, or playing around.

I remember standing outside of Jester Dormitory my sophomore year, waiting for my friend to pick me up so we could go out to eat at IHOP. I gazed across the street and through the basement window of the PCL. There was Joseph with headphones on, his notebook open, taking notes from his textbook. He was putting forth effort—doing the best he could, even when he did not have to.

I prayed to graduate from the University of Texas with a 3.0 GPA, and that is exactly what I earned. Joseph, on the other hand, combined his intelligence with consistent effort and graduated with all A's except for one B, which gave him a 3.9 GPA. He graduated in the top 1 percent of his class. Later, he completed a graduate degree at Harvard and has excelled in every role he has had because he learned early on that talent is not enough. You need effort to maximize talent. I am grateful for his example.

Joseph is my personal example of effort, but I also love to study people who have maximized their talents with effort. Kobe Bryant would bring everyone into the gym and practice for hours after everyone was gone. LeBron James has played professional basketball for 22 years at the time of this book. He, like Kobe, was a phenomenal player in high school, but many have had potential that didn't pan out to long-term success. LeBron has been known to invest over 1 million dollars a year in his body through nutrition, training, and recovery. He shoots thousands of shots a day and studies the game as if he's playing every position. His talent would have taken him to the league, but his effort has allowed him to become the all-time leading scorer in NBA history, having played more than the equivalent of three 82-game seasons in the playoffs, including 10 finals appearances and 4 NBA championships. He doesn't just excel during the games; he loves the process of preparation and practice.

Every morning, you should wake up committing to putting in your best effort for the day that you've received as a gift. Every night, you should ask yourself if I did the best I could today, even when I didn't have to. History makers put forth effort privately when no one is looking so they can excel when history calls publicly. I challenge you to adopt a mindset of maximum effort today and see how your life begins to make history in the lives of those around you.

CHAPTER 6
EXPECTATIONS
Learning to manage your expectations

Expectations are often an underrated factor when we study history makers. Early on in my career, I developed what I describe as the expectation equation.

High Expectation + High Outcome = Satisfaction

When I worked at Kmart during the summer before my senior year, I was hired to make $8 an hour and worked an average of 20 hours a week. So I expected to make $160 a week. When my expectation met my outcome, I was satisfied.

High Expectation + Higher Outcome = Surprise

When I worked my typical 20-hour week and received $180 due to an unexpected bonus, my outcome exceeded my expectations, and I was surprised. Let's say I had $20 worth of surprise.

High Expectation + Low Outcome = Disappointment

When I worked my first 20-hour week after starting the job, I expected to make $160. I already had plans for how I was going to give my $16 tithe and take my girlfriend to Chick-fil-A and a movie. I was ready to buy my mom a gift for praying for me to get the job. I was even thinking about sending my brother $20 so he could get something he wanted while at college.

I didn't know that Kmart—and many other employers at that time—would hold your first week's check. They called it "having a check in the hole." I had never heard of such a thing. Needless to say, I was disappointed, because the $160 I expected to be in my pocket was in a hole somewhere that I couldn't find. I'm a little dramatic, but you get my point. I wanted what I expected.

If you're going to make history in your lifetime, you have to learn how to manage your expectations.

When you look at the equation, there are three components:

- **Expectations** (high or low)
- **Outcomes** (high or low)
- **Response** (satisfied, surprised, or disappointed)

How do you manage your expectations? You manage them by understanding what to expect in specific situations. During a morning commute, if you expect there to be traffic, you won't be disappointed when you encounter it. You have planned to take more time to get to work; you have planned to listen to your favorite artist or a new audiobook. You have prepared your hot coffee and favorite breakfast bar. You have prepared for the outcome, so you are not disappointed. If you arrive early, you are surprised, and if you arrive on time, you are satisfied. You are not disappointed, because you expected traffic.

We live in a culture of unspoken expectations. You may know what you expect, but how often do you express those expectations? Unspoken expectations usually lead to unmet expectations and rarely exceed expectations. Much of the disappointment you feel throughout the day stems from expectations left unspoken.

We also live in a culture of unrealistic expectations. The rise of social media and access to others' lives creates an unrealistic idea of what life should be. Remember that your friends on social media are showing you their highlights, not their lowlights. Your friends are showing their touchdowns, not their turnovers. Never get it twisted; life has ups and downs. History makers learn how to manage their expectations so they don't get overwhelmed by this reality.

I've never been on a cruise ship, but I have been on a speedboat, and when the boat moves in ways I don't expect, I get seasick. I may not actually vomit, but I feel sick the whole trip because of unmanaged expectations about speed, direction, temperature, or simple, necessary hydration. If I check the weather, study the route, and connect with someone who has been through it before, I can develop a realistic expectation, so I am either satisfied or pleasantly surprised.

The Rev. Dr. Alex Gee has been someone in my life who has kept me from getting seasick on the journey of ministry, racial reconciliation, and community development. I first heard Alex Gee speak at Urbana 2000, an international missions conference hosted by InterVarsity Christian Fellowship. I sat in the mezzanine of Assembly Hall on the University of Illinois at Urbana–Champaign campus as he shared a vision for racial reconciliation in the Christian church in America that I longed for.

As I shared, I grew up in Abilene, Texas, a city that was significantly segregated by race when it came to churches. My two best friends were white and Hispanic. We did everything together during the week, but worshiped in racially segregated churches. I now know why the churches were segregated based on the history of the church in America, but at the time, I was disappointed because I thought my community would be better than that. I dreamed of a day when all my friends could worship together in a church where our cultures would be accepted and affirmed, instead of having to acquiesce and assimilate.

Alex began preaching as a teenager and was quickly placed in spiritual leadership in his Black Pentecostal church. As he spent time in Madison, Wisconsin, matriculating through the educational system, including the University of Wisconsin–Madison, he developed as a community leader. Over time, his church became more multiethnic, and he began to build relationships with leaders such as Steve Hayner, president of InterVarsity Christian Fellowship. Through personal relationships, the vision for reconciliation in the Christian church became the focus of Alex's ministry. By the time I met him, I had begun to believe that racial reconciliation was possible.

In the summer of 2001, I came on staff with InterVarsity, planting a fellowship to minister to Black students at the University of Texas. We also had fellowships reaching Asian American, South Asian (Indian), and Latino students. The goal of each fellowship was to provide a safe place for students to be formed and affirmed in their ethnic identity while growing in their relationship with God.

In the summer of 2002, nearly three hundred students from our region met for our leadership camp at Camp Buckner in Marble Falls, Texas. Our fellowship had only seven students represented, so we felt outnumbered and out of place in this new model of ministry that was primarily white, contemplative, and conservative. The regional leadership team felt it was important for the Black students who were new to InterVarsity to feel accepted and affirmed as they joined the ministry, so they invited Alex and his worship team to lead our main sessions. During that time, Alex became a mentor to me in racial reconciliation.

While we were connecting after a session in his cabin, he told me, "Corey, I know you're the first Black staff member in this region, and your fellowship has a small representation here. These students and staff need you to be the Black man God created you to be. If you show up but don't bring who you are to the table, you are denying them the gift of who God created you to be." This was important for me to hear, because up to that point, I often assimilated into the majority culture to fit in. I wanted to be accepted so I could advance, and I figured that once I got into leadership, I could make changes to help others, but I didn't think I could get there while being fully myself.

He helped me change my expectations for how I needed to show up. He also helped me manage my expectations for how other races would perceive me as a Black man. So when I did something that was Black and not the normal tradition within the movement, I knew it would take time for people to adjust, but through our faith in Christ, I knew they could.

My first encounter with him was twenty-five years ago, and to this day we have both been living out these principles of the expectation equation in our roles as spiritual and community leaders. Since that time, I have spoken in churches of many different racial backgrounds, served as chaplain of the Republican Party of Texas, been appointed to the OneStar National Service Commission, and served on the board of Texas Alliance for Life. I have led a pregnancy center as the sexual risk avoidance education program director serving mostly white students, and I have launched a multicultural church. Each of these roles gave me an opportunity to manage my expectations while building bridges with people who differed from me culturally.

Alex has now led Fountain of Life Covenant Church for over forty years, founded and developed the Nehemiah Center for Urban Leadership Development, and written two books: *Jesus and the Hip Hop Prophets: Spiritual Insights from Lauryn Hill and 2Pac* and *When God Lets You Down: Trusting Again After Pain and Loss*. He hosts a podcast called *Black Like Me*, on which I have been featured, and he has been a mentor to leaders across the globe.

On December 8, 2013, Alex wrote an op-ed in *The Capital Times* (Madison, Wisconsin) entitled "Justified Anger." In the article, he recounts the disappointment he felt when a white woman approached him after speaking at a Rotary meeting and said, "Wonderful presentation, Dr. Gee! If you don't mind, I must tell you that I am so glad that you are not some angry Black man!"

Alex writes, "This well-intentioned white Rotarian had just heard how Wisconsin has an epidemic and leads the nation in the incarceration of African American males between 20 and 24 years old.

"Giving these kinds of presentations typically takes a toll on me because of the bleakness of the subject matter, the pain in my soul unearthed by the topic, and the typically blank stares by people who wonder why we are still talking about racial disparities in 2013.

"'I am an angry Black man,' I responded. 'Why would you think I wasn't angry over what is happening in and to my community? Is it because I put on my best face and "safe" Black voice for you today?'"

Alex went on to describe the multiple times he has been racially profiled around his church, which has several police officers as parishioners. He was extremely disappointed in her statement and in the state of his city, but he did not let that stop him.

After the article was published, the city began to respond, and Alex led another movement. In 2015, the Nehemiah Center for Urban Leadership Development launched its Justified Anger initiative to engage thousands of non-Black allies in addressing racism by understanding and seeking to change the systems that hold it in place. People from across the city began coming to Fountain of Life Covenant Church, where Nehemiah taught its renowned "Black History for a New Day" course, equipping non-Black allies with Black history that would allow them to respond with insight, empathy, and empowerment. The Nehemiah Center offers other courses, including its "Why History Matters" series—such as *Systemic Racism in Higher Education and Society* and *Slavery and Capitalism.*

Nehemiah created "Our Madison Plan," a ten-year vision for empowering and uplifting the African American community in Madison. As I write, Alex Gee and Nehemiah have raised nearly thirty million dollars to establish and build the Center for Black Excellence and Culture, a space designed to bring together collective Black brilliance to affirm, inspire, and advance the Black community in Madison and beyond. The center will focus on:

- Health and wellness
- Leadership and innovation
- Performing and visual arts
- Youth and families

This 65,000-square-foot destination will be a landmark in the region, with both cultural impact and physical imprint, demonstrating the power of leadership and community partnerships. Annually, the center will teach 6,000 students Black history, host 8,000 people for Black performances and art, welcome 3,000 seniors for wisdom and experience sharing, and support 175 members of the Center for Black Innovation and Leadership.

Alex has demonstrated that disappointment—shown through unmet expectations—can lead to invitations to others that exceed your expectations. I am not surprised that Alex has led this movement, because Alex is a leader of leaders, but I am a little surprised by how many of our white brothers and sisters have come under his leadership to execute this vision. In our nation, Black people often sit under and follow white leaders, but we do not have a long history of non-Black people choosing to follow Black leadership. Just look at the disparities in city, state, and national governments. Look at the disparities in our institutions of higher learning and churches. It is often subtle and subconscious, but it is a reality.

Alex has exceeded all expectations and is leading with conviction and dignity, which honors God and inspires people.

If you would like to learn more about Alex Gee and his work, you can visit the following websites:

- www.alexgee.com
- www.nehemiah.org
- www.theblackcenter.org

Alex and I have both been bridge builders as we have made history. We have learned to build bridges between communities with racial differences, gender differences, and even economic differences, but that comes at a cost. Dr. Soong-Chan Rah is the Robert Boyd Munger Professor of Evangelism at Fuller Seminary, Pasadena, California. Years ago, I heard him share this poignant truth: "The challenge with being a bridge builder is that you often get walked on from both sides. Many in the Black community cannot understand why Alex and I would do the work to build bridges or serve with those who can be, and have been, oppressive to our people. We do it because we expect that someone like us can make a difference for our children and our children's children. We want to create a better community for future generations, and we are willing to pay the cost."

Most people miss their moment in history because unmet expectations cause them to give up too soon or become distracted from the main goal. I encourage you to let the expectation equation multiply your impact today and for years to come, so you too can make history in your lifetime.

CHAPTER 7
EDUCATION
Learning how to learn

Growing up, I was always encouraged to get a good education. As I advanced through different school levels, I realized that getting a "good education" and being educated are two different things. You cannot truly be educated at a great institution—or get a "good education"—if you have not learned how to learn.

When I arrived at the University of Texas, I saw the difference between having a "good education" and being educated. In high school, I completed honors chemistry my senior year and earned straight A's. I enjoyed learning the periodic table and working with a partner in the lab. I had a good time and realized that science was not my enemy; it could be my friend.

I enrolled in a freshman chemistry course at UT, and the class covered everything we had learned in a semester within the first two days. From then on, I was learning chemistry from a professor who fully understood the material but struggled to teach it effectively to students who were not chemistry majors. For pre-med, biochemistry, and other natural science students, his teaching made sense. For me— an elementary education major taking the course only because it was required—it made little sense. This was the first time I realized that being educated means learning how to learn.

When I graduated, I began working at the freshman admissions center for the University of Texas at Austin. My job title was freshman admissions advisor. Most college admissions advisors travel around the state or the country, exhibiting at college fairs and visiting high school campuses. They spend a great deal of time connecting with high school guidance counselors to meet a quota of students who apply and ultimately choose their university. My role was different: I stayed in Austin and worked in John Hargis Hall, our freshman admissions office. I recruited current students to host prospective students who came to visit the campus.

We would bring busloads of students from areas such as Dallas–Fort Worth, Houston, and the Rio Grande Valley. I would have a team of student volunteers ready to meet them and guide them during their campus tour, class visits, and meal times in the cafeteria. The goal was to give the students a taste of the campus experience and allow them to speak with current students who were living the student life. Since I had already graduated, I was no longer as strong a witness to the current student experience. Instead, I was an example of what could happen once you graduate.

Within my first week in the role, I learned how important education—learning how to learn—is after graduation. The courses I took in college were not necessarily designed to translate every fact or concept directly into my job. Instead, my degree demonstrated that I could finish what I started and that I knew how to learn. Whatever role you enter after college, the company or organization will take you through an orientation and teach you what they want you to know and how they want you to do your job. If you have not learned how to learn, you will struggle to gain the insights needed to be effective.

In the same way, my entire high school honors chemistry class was covered in two days of college instruction; your college education will likely be condensed into the first week of a new job. From then on, you are learning the company's model and path to success.

If education isn't just knowing information but learning how to learn, how do you become educated?

You become educated by learning **how you learn**. Once you learn how to learn, you can learn anything. Various organizations have studied learning styles. You will hear about models of learning styles, which include:

- **Visual learners** thrive when information is presented through images, diagrams, charts, and other visuals. They benefit from mind maps, graphic organizers, and using color-coded notes.
- **Auditory learners** process information through listening. They often enjoy lectures, discussions, and podcasts. They may also benefit from reading aloud or recording information to review later.
- **Kinesthetic learners** learn by doing and experiencing. They prefer hands-on activities, experiments, and physical demonstrations. They may benefit from using manipulatives, building models, or role-playing.
- **Reading/Writing learners** excel when information is presented in written form. They often enjoy textbooks, articles, and note-taking. They may also benefit from summarizing information in their own words or creating outlines.

As you can imagine, knowing your primary and secondary learning styles gives you an advantage. If you are a visual learner, you can turn any information into a diagram to learn it better. If you are an auditory learner, you might choose an audiobook over a printed book. If you are a reading/writing learner, you may read the physical book and then create your own outlines. If you are a kinesthetic learner, you will create a model or activity to engage your learning process.

Learning how you learn is the key to unlocking the knowledge available to us through education. Once you learn how you learn, you can learn anything. If you are interested in gaining more insight into your learning style, you can complete the VARK learning-styles self-assessment.

In addition to the VARK styles, four other learning preferences are often referenced in education:

- **Logical (analytical/mathematical) learners** thrive on problem-solving. They enjoy finding solutions to complex problems.
- **Interpersonal (social) learners** thrive through collaboration. They enjoy small-group discussions or group projects and often learn by teaching or discussing with others.
- **Intrapersonal (solo) learners** thrive through independent study and reflection. They prefer

time alone to learn and to reflect without distractions.

- **Naturalistic learners** thrive when nature is incorporated into learning, studying outdoors, or using natural examples to connect concepts.

There is no wrong way to learn. We are all wired to learn in certain ways. The challenge is that our educational system often leans toward specific methods that do not serve all students. For example, sitting still in straight rows and listening to a ninety-minute lecture rarely works for social or kinesthetic learners. If the lecture has slides, the visual learner can follow some models, but the kinesthetic learner may end up doodling or fidgeting simply to stay engaged as the lecture continues.

As a speaker and coach, I can lecture, but the key to unlocking education for my clients is speaking to their learning styles. Many teachers teach only in their own style and miss much of their audience. It takes work and intentionality to teach to four, let alone eight, learning styles, but it is possible. The key is to create your message and then review it through the different styles. You may want to use a symbol or emoji for each style and assess your manuscript to see how it measures up.

Booker T. Washington grew up in a time when formal education was not available to Black people in

America, particularly in the former Confederate South. He was born into slavery on a tobacco plantation on April 5, 1856, in Hales Ford, Virginia. He was freed at nine years old when U.S. troops reached the area during the Civil War. He worked his way through Hampton Normal and Agricultural Institute and attended Wayland Seminary. He often said that Black people needed to educate themselves, learn useful trades, and invest in their own businesses, and he committed himself to all three. His autobiography, *Up from Slavery*, became a best seller, and he started what is now known as Tuskegee University in Tuskegee, Alabama. He hired George Washington Carver to teach agriculture at Tuskegee Institute in 1896. Carver went on to develop hundreds of food, industrial, and commercial products from peanuts, including milk substitutes, sauces, cooking oils, soaps, and wood stains.

As we conclude this chapter, I want to affirm those who have struggled with traditional formal education. Just because someone was not able, or chose not, to teach to your learning style does not mean you cannot learn. You can learn once you learn how you learn. So I encourage you to do the work, identify your learning styles, and use them to your advantage.

CHAPTER 8

EXPERIENCE

Engaging in experiences that maximize your education

While I was in college, I knew I wanted to graduate with at least a 3.0 GPA, but I was committed to engaging in extracurricular activities, student organizations, and strategic work opportunities that would allow me to maximize my education. One of my first experiences at the University of Texas was going to orientation the summer before I started school. During orientation, I saw staff who worked in student affairs and led the orientation experience, and I met older students who were serving as orientation advisors. They provided us with insights on how to prepare for the college experience through talks, skits, and academic advising.

As soon as I saw what they were doing, I said, "I want to do that in a couple of years." The summers after my sophomore and junior years, I served as an orientation advisor; in fact, I was selected as an outstanding orientation advisor both years. I loved this job because it allowed me to take what I was learning in the classroom and gain experience to maximize that education. From leading campus tours to giving presentations and offering academic advising, I was in my sweet spot. I was using skills I had, and I was building on them for my educational experience. Many of the students who came into the university at that time became my little brothers and sisters on campus. I have seen them go on to become doctors, lawyers, professors, journalists, dentists, pastors; you name it. I am happy to have been part of the process, and I gained so much from them during that time.

I also served in the Innervisions Gospel Choir as chaplain and later president for three years. Over my five years in the choir, I learned how to lead naturally and spiritually, which equipped me to be a better campus minister and, later, a staff pastor and church planter. I learned how to make mistakes and recover from them so that failure is no longer a fear but a factor to gain information about what I should do next. I learned to prioritize my purpose when my at-large student government position became too much to balance with my role as president of the choir; I chose the choir. I navigated writing and producing our first album, and I attended national conferences and regional performances. All that I learned in the choir prepared me for what I am doing today.

I joined Gamma Phi Delta Christian Fraternity, Inc., during my freshman year. I was mentored by Donyall Dickey, a journalism major. He taught me how to dress, how to carry myself with confidence, and the value of integrity. He asked me hard questions about my relationships and modeled what I could be as a Black man on UT's campus. He taught me graphic design, a tool I use weekly in my work today.

Donyall went on to complete a doctorate in education and founded one of the most effective educational literacy and consulting companies in the nation, Educational Epiphany. He served as an administrator in schools and school districts. He saw the need for effective literacy tools to help children read. Throughout our nation, states have been said to plan prison capacity using indicators such as reading skills; if a student is not reading at grade level by the third grade, the state may factor that into estimates of how many jail cells will be needed.

Donyall and his team create resources that help students learn to read, which is a gift to our community. His students may or may not know Dr. Seuss, but they all know Dr. Dickey because he helped them learn how to read. He travels the country delivering keynotes at educational conferences and professional development workshops, and he builds tools that districts across the country use daily with their students. Donyall is making history in his lifetime because he matched his education with experience, and it is proving to be life-changing for many.

While in college, I served as a resident assistant, hosting programs for students in my dormitory. Today, I host events for my organization and at my home for our church all the time. It was not enough to get a classroom education if I wanted to make history in my lifetime; I had to match the education with experience, because often more is caught than taught.

I graduated from UT with 144 credit hours, having changed my major four times. Most students graduate with 120 credit hours after changing their major, possibly once. I changed from elementary education after two years to magazine journalism, then to corporate communication, and finally to communication studies. I went from wanting to be a teacher, to wanting to create a magazine, to wanting to own the magazine, to wanting to be a Christian counselor.

I know parents do not want to hear this, but 75 percent of students change their major at least once while in college, because it is really hard to know what you want to do when you are eighteen years old and have not been exposed to the many available options. College allows for much of that exposure while a student is eighteen to twenty-two years old.

Every major change I made was because of an experience I had outside the classroom. Growing up, I wanted to be the Black male elementary teacher I had never had. I did not have a Black teacher until I went to college. I knew that many students in urban schools did not have fathers in their lives, so I wanted to be a father figure they could look up to. UT had a program called Neighborhood Longhorns. I became an after-school volunteer and quickly realized that I could teach (lecture) all day long, but I could not handle the classroom management required to be an elementary school teacher, so after two years, I changed my major.

I was attending a prominent neo-Pentecostal church in Austin that was founded by an amazing preacher and theologian, Dr. Dana Carson. He was a success story in his own right, having dropped out of high school in Chicago and later completing his required credits in an alternative learning program. He went on to complete a Bachelor's in Business Administration at Wiley College in East Texas, and, while planting Praise Tabernacle Church, he completed his Master of Divinity at Austin Presbyterian Theological Seminary and Oral Roberts University, and his Doctor of

Ministry at Boston University. The church attracted many college students and young professionals because of its combination of spiritual vigor and intellectually rigorous teaching.

I'd never met a pastor who was theologically trained and worked as a pastor full-time. The teaching was powerful, and the music ministry was breathtaking. Coming from a small family church to this megachurch was eye-opening for me. I thought I should create a magazine that featured people like Dr. Carson and churches like Praise Tabernacle. Surely there was a market for people to learn about this kind of church, to aspire to it, or to grow through its example.

While taking my first journalism class with Dr. Marvin Olasky, founder and editor of *World* magazine, I realized I didn't want to write the magazine. I wanted to own the magazine. I wanted to run a business. By that point—three years into my education—it was too late to enter the highly competitive McCombs School of Business at UT. So I decided to do the next best thing: earn a minor in business through the Business Foundations certificate. I completed one class in each business discipline while majoring in corporate communication. I enjoyed my business classes, but soon realized I didn't want to run the magazine as much as I wanted to help people.

As president of the gospel choir and a member of the Christian fraternity, I often counseled choir members and fraternity brothers about their relationships. I had a knack for relationships because I studied them so hard in hopes of being in a good one myself. Though I dated in high school and college, I often felt out of my league, so I studied relationships intentionally. As I helped couples with their relationships and students with their fears about classes and challenges with their parents, I thought I should become a Christian counselor. I changed my major to communication studies with an emphasis on human relations because it was too late to go back for a psychology degree; plus, I had struggled in my only psychology class up to that point.

My goal was to finish my degree—now on a five-year plan—and then attend Dallas Theological Seminary to complete a Master of Arts in Counseling. During my fifth year, I worked as a peer counselor in the Career Exploration Center. Between my studies in human relations and my work at the center, I learned about personality assessments, career assessments, and how to use these tools to help people. I had multiple one-on-one appointments with students each day I worked.

I soon realized that Corey, the extrovert, could not handle that many one-on-one appointments.

It wore me out. As an extrovert, I gain energy from people, more like small groups and medium to large groups. Introverts gain energy from being alone but often thrive in one-on-one conversations. I began to imagine what my days would be like as a counselor with five to seven appointments daily; I would not be happy. So I committed to finishing this degree, but I was no longer sure counseling was for me.

While I was in college, I knew I wanted to graduate with at least a 3.0 GPA, but I was committed to engaging in extracurricular activities, student organizations, and strategic work opportunities that would allow me to maximize my education. I decided to stay in Austin for a year after graduating and took a job at the freshman admissions center. While working there, I started teaching a Bible study on Tuesday nights called "The Real World." I taught students who were one to three years younger than I was. Some students could not make it on Tuesday nights, so I began another study on my lunch break on Wednesdays. I could not get enough of working with students, helping them apply Scripture to daily life and discover how to live out their purpose in light of their faith. I was on a path to my future.

During my third and fourth years of school, I met weekly for lunch with David Hanke, the campus minister with InterVarsity Christian Fellowship. We talked about life as Christian men who wanted to honor God with our lives. He was married to his wife, Laurel; I was dating and trying to make sense of the relationship I was in and where my life was headed. Over time, I saw that he spent his days helping college students figure out their faith. He invited me to attend a Black student conference in Atlanta, Georgia, where I met others who did the same work he did, and I met students from across the country who were serious about their faith. Someone recommended I attend a conference that InterVarsity offered triennially called Urbana. It was an international missions conference held at the University of Illinois at Urbana-Champaign, hence the name *Urbana*.

Two other students and I attended that conference from December 27 to 31, 2000. While there, I saw nearly twenty thousand students from across the country and the world seeking God's heart for their future. I met Dr. Brenda Salter McNeil, who clarified my purpose while I was giving a short talk in the Black student lounge. I heard Dr. Alex Gee speak from his heart about racial reconciliation and fulfilling God's call on one's life. During my time there I sensed clearly that I was supposed to enter full-time ministry with InterVarsity to launch a ministry serving Black students at the University of Texas. I was nervous because I knew I would need to raise financial support, and I had not seen that work well for many of my Black friends. But I could also see how my childhood in Abilene, with two best friends who were white and Hispanic, had prepared me to build bridges on campus while developing a ministry where Black students could grow in their ethnic identity and in their faith.

When I got home from this amazing conference, I shared my passion with my girlfriend, April, now my wife, and with my pastor, Dr. Carson, and he affirmed it. Soon I turned in my notice to resign from the admissions office and began serving as the first African American campus staff member with InterVarsity in what is now the Red River Region. At the time, we were just Texas, but now the region includes Texas, Oklahoma, Louisiana, and Arkansas.

I attended new staff orientation in Madison, Wisconsin, and came home to start raising support. Campus ministers invite people in their community to donate monthly, quarterly, or annually to fund the ministry budget, which includes salary, benefits, ministry expenses, and overhead. I needed to raise about $50,000 to make around $25,000 a year. I enjoyed sharing the vision of what God was calling us to do, and I enjoyed meeting with so many people to talk about it. I did one-on-one dinners, couples hosted dessert gatherings in their homes with five to seven couples, and I spoke at churches to share the work we were doing.

On September 11, 2001, we were preparing to host our first large group. At that time, we had about seven students who were committed to Bible study and serving as leaders. That morning, planes flew into the Twin Towers in New York City, and we had a decision to make. The country was in crisis, and we had already waited nearly three weeks into the semester to start. We did not think we could wait any longer. The university hosted a candlelight vigil at the Main Tower that evening. We sent the seven students there to pray and invite others to Bible study. They came back with forty others. We were off to an amazing start.

Weekly, I taught topics like relationships, spiritual disciplines, finances, academics, and purpose within the context of our Christian faith. The ministry grew by leaps and bounds. On October 9, I proposed to April at the study, and by the spring semester, we were seeing nearly one hundred students a week. Over the next four years, more than five hundred students came through the ministry. I saw students who dated and are now married with children. I saw students who led small groups and are now business leaders and pastors. I saw students who sang on the worship team and now work in television and education.

I didn't know it, but we were making history in our lifetime. From seven students going to the Main Tower for a candlelight vigil to seven students attending leadership camp that summer, this ministry to Black students in the Red River Region has grown exponentially. In November 2024, I attended a regional Black Campus Ministries conference known as Catalyst. There were more than 150 Black students present, representing hundreds of Black students engaged in InterVarsity ministries on various campuses, including historically Black colleges and universities (HBCUs) and predominantly white institutions (PWIs).

I had no idea that my decision to start teaching a Bible study on a Tuesday night would lead me to serve in full-time ministry for more than twenty years. But it didn't start that Tuesday night; it started in 1985, when my children's minister invited me to teach Bible study to six-year-olds when I was eight years old because I could read. My purpose was developed early through experience.

You can go to class and earn a 4.0 GPA, but if you do not find a way to match experiences with your education, you will miss the moment to make the biggest impact you can—serving other people through the gifts and abilities you have. Maki

CHAPTER 9
CONCLUSION
Start Making History Today

History is just his story or her story, and it is shared with others over time through the stories we tell our children and grandchildren, as well as the stories we hear from our parents and grandparents. History makers create stories that others hear because what they have accomplished echoes into the lives of those who tell their stories. I did not have time in this book to share all the people who have made history in my lifetime, much less the history of our nation and the world, but I promise you will find these principles lived out in each of their lives.

Seven Principles for Making History

1. **Decision:** the ability to say yes.
2. **Discipline:** the ability to say no so you can say yes to something else.
3. **Excellence:** doing the best you can with what you have.

4. **Effort:** doing the best you can, even when you do not have to.

5. **Expectation:** managing your expectations so you are satisfied or surprised more often than disappointed.

6. **Education:** learning how to learn.

7. **Experience:** engaging in experiences that maximize your education.

Think of someone in history, and you will see these seven principles lived out. Here is my challenge to you: consider how you are already making history. You may be the first in your family to go to college or the first in your family to stay married. You may be the first person of your gender or race to win a political office in your community or the first to launch a STEM program where you live. Making history does not always mean you are the first to do it; it may mean you are the next to do it. Perhaps you grab the baton from a leader who has served well and build on their legacy. Perhaps you take the pain of your family's past and build toward a better future. You can make history in your lifetime.

Soon after, April and I joined Greater Mt. Zion Baptist Church in Austin, Texas, under the leadership of Pastor Gaylon Clark, and I was invited to preach on October 1, 2003. We had just been married in June and joined the church in August. Pastor Clark had to travel out of town for the funeral of a church member, and I preached a sermon entitled "Legacy or Liability: What Will Your Mark Be."

My economics class at UT taught me that there are assets that gain value over time and leave a legacy for future family members, and there are liabilities that cost more than they make and erode or limit legacy for future generations. Some assets cost greatly on the front end but produce even more on the back end. Many liabilities cost greatly on the front end and never produce value on the back. The point of the message was to challenge each member of the church to consider, when they leave the church—whether by transferring to another church, moving to another city, or dying and going to heaven—what their mark will be: legacy or liability.

I shared the illustration that in the graveyards of our world, there is a headstone at each plot listing the name of the person, typically given by their parents; the birth date and death date, which I believe were given by God; and the dash between those two dates. Some dashes are long, with over one hundred years of life, and some dashes are short, with less than a day of life. I have buried and preached at funerals of family members who were nearly one hundred years old, and I have buried children who were stillborn.

I believe that each of our lives has a purpose, and what we do with our dash matters. No one lying on a deathbed thinks about how big a house they had or how much money they had in the bank. No one thinks about how many hours they work at their job or how many cars they own. The final thought of each person who has passed from this life to the next is what they did with their dash and, most importantly, the lives they impacted and the people they loved.

Making history in your lifetime is about living a life that lasts beyond yours. It is about being remembered for a smile or a hug when someone really needed it, or a compliment and affirmation when someone was considering giving up. Your historical moment might be the decision to say yes to taking less for a job that would lead to making an impact later. I do not know where you are in your journey, but I want to challenge you to choose history today so your story is told later.

I am only forty-eight years old, but I have seen history unfold in my nearly half-century. I believe it is the foundation for the history I hope to build over the next forty to fifty years. My wife and my children are the most important storytellers in my life. I want them to be able to say I had a husband who loved me for me and made room for me to grow into who I was created to be. I want my daughters to say they had a dad who modeled greatness through service and hospitality.

After my children, my faith community, and my local community have motivated me to make history. I want my faith community to say I loved God with all my heart and demonstrated my love through how I used my gifts and abilities to add value. I want my local community to say I cared, supported community leaders, and filled in the gaps when asked. I want my coworkers and associates to say I made them feel they could do it, even when others said they could not. I want them to know that I believed in them and would do anything I could to help them get to their next.

When I die, whenever that is, I want God to say, "Well done, good and faithful servant; you have been faithful over a few things; I will make you ruler over many. Come and share in your master's joy" (Matthew 25:23). This is what I am living for, and this is how I want to live until the day I die. Prayerfully, this is how I will be remembered.

Study Guide

Putting the 7 keys into practice

1. Discipline

   What do you need to say yes to at this season in your life?

   _____

   _____

   _____

2. Decision

   What do you need to say no to so you can say yes in this season in your life?

   _____

   _____

   _____

3. Excellence

   What do you currently have that you can do the best within this season in your life?

   _____

   _____

   _____

4. Effort

   In what area do you need to put forth more effort this season in your life?

   _____

   _____

   _____

5. Expectation

What expectations do you need to manage more effectively during this season of your life?

_____

_____

_____

6. Education

How do you need to grow in learning to learn in this season in your life?

_____

_____

_____

7. Experience

In what experience(s) do you need to engage to maximize your education?

_____

_____

_____

_____

Life Reflection Questions

Writing your story

1. What do you wish someone had told you when you were a child to prepare you to be a history maker in your lifetime?

   _____

   _____

   _____

2. Who are the children you could share that with today?

   _____

   _____

   _____

3. What do you want your family to say about you when you're gone?

   _____

   _____

   _____

4. What do you want your friends to say about you when you're gone?

   _____

   _____

   _____

5. What do you want your co-workers or colleagues to say about you when you're gone?

_____

_____

_____

6. What do you want your neighbors to say about you when you're gone?

_____

_____

_____

7. What is something you've always wanted to do but were too scared to do it?

_____

_____

_____

8. What is keeping you from doing it now?

_____

_____

_____

9. What help do you need to enlist to accomplish this dream?

_____

_____

_____

10. What are you willing to sacrifice to accomplish your dream?

_____

_____

_____

11. What will you forfeit if you don't pursue your dream?

_____

_____

_____

12. What's the worst thing that could happen if you pursue your dream?

_____

_____

_____

13. What's the best thing that could happen if you pursue your dream?

_____

_____

_____

14. What dreams have you already accomplished that could encourage you on the journey? (List at least 5)

1. _____

2. _____

3. _____

4. _____

5. _____

15. Are you willing to die without pursuing your
    dream?

    _____

    _____

    _____

These are questions I ask myself daily, monthly, quarterly, and annually. In my book *Prioritize for Your Purpose: Ordering Your Life to Be Extraordinary*, I discuss ways to discover your purpose and prioritize your roles, relationships, time, and money to accomplish it. Your purpose will not be fulfilled by accident. Your dream will not become a reality by accident. You have to be intentional. Asking yourself these questions—and being honest with yourself—will help you begin moving toward a life story that will be remembered.

If you need support in this area, I am Corey Tabor, the purpose partner. I inform, instruct, and inspire people to fulfill their purpose. You can connect with me at www.coreytabor.com for speaking, writing, and coaching services. Let's make history in our lifetime.

Corey Tabor is a dynamic speaker, author, and life coach. He is the Founder and President of III Coaching, which is a coaching firm that informs, instructs, and inspires others to fulfill their purpose.

Corey graduated from the University of Texas at Austin with a B.S. in Communication Studies / Human Relations with a minor in Business. He also completed a Masters of Ministry Leadership from Rockbridge Seminary.

Corey has served in various roles throughout his career, leading faith-based nonprofits, including InterVarsity Christian Fellowship, Greater Mt. Zion Church Austin, Full Life Community Church, Pflugerville, The Source Austin, BiG Austin, Apartment Life, and Care Net.

Corey has spoken for distinguished groups such as The University of Texas at Austin Football Team, The Southwestern Black Student Leadership Conference at Texas A&M, The Impact Movement, The Texas Campaign to Prevent Teen Pregnancy Summit, The

National Society of Black Engineers, as well as various churches throughout the country.

In addition to his academic degrees, Corey has multiple certifications, including:

1. Maxwell Leadership Certified - Maxwell Institute
2. Human Behavior Specialist – Uniquely You
3. Professional Life Coach – Fowler International Academy of Professional Coaching
4. Certificate in Nonprofit Leadership and Management – Austin Community College

Corey has been married to his wife, April, since 2003, and they have 2 children, Anaia and Charis.

You can follow his work or book him at **www. coreytabor.com**

www.ingramcontent.com/pod-product-compliance
Lightning Source LLC
Chambersburg PA
CBHW021126130626
46554CB00002B/884